addresses

D1298745

PETER PAUPER PRESS, INC.
WHITE PLAINS, NEW YORK

PETER PAUPER PRESS
Fine Books and Gifts Since 1928

Our Company

In 1928, at the age of twenty-two, Peter Beilenson began printing books on a small press in the basement of his parents' home in Larchmont, New York. Peter—and later his wife, Edna—sought to create fine books that sold at "prices even a pauper could afford."

Today, still family owned and operated, Peter Pauper Press continues to honor our founders' legacy—and our customers' expectations—of beauty, quality, and value.

Designed by Margaret Rubiano

Copyright © 2014
Peter Pauper Press, Inc.
202 Mamaroneck Avenue
White Plains, NY 10601
All rights reserved
ISBN 978-1-4413-1532-8
Printed in Hong Kong
7 6 5 4 3 2

Visit us at www.peterpauper.com

addresses

NAME

ADDRESS

HOME

MOBILE

WORK / FAX

E-MAIL

NAME

ADDRESS

HOME

MOBILE

WORK / FAX

E-MAIL

NAME

ADDRESS

HOME

MOBILE

WORK / FAX

E-MAIL

NAME

ADDRESS

HOME

MOBILE

WORK / FAX

E-MAIL

NAME

ADDRESS

HOME

MOBILE

WORK / FAX

E-MAIL

NAME

ADDRESS

HOME

MOBILE

WORK / FAX

E-MAIL

NAME

ADDRESS

HOME

MOBILE

WORK / FAX

E-MAIL

NAME

ADDRESS

HOME

MOBILE

WORK / FAX

E-MAIL

NAME

ADDRESS

HOME

MOBILE

WORK / FAX

E-MAIL

NAME

ADDRESS

HOME

MOBILE

WORK / FAX

E-MAIL

NAME

ADDRESS

HOME

MOBILE

WORK / FAX

E-MAIL

NAME

ADDRESS

HOME

MOBILE

WORK / FAX

E-MAIL

NAME

ADDRESS

HOME

MOBILE

WORK / FAX

E-MAIL

NAME

ADDRESS

HOME

MOBILE

WORK / FAX

E-MAIL

NAME

ADDRESS

HOME

MOBILE

WORK / FAX

E-MAIL

NAME

ADDRESS

HOME

MOBILE

WORK / FAX

E-MAIL

NAME

ADDRESS

HOME

MOBILE

WORK / FAX

E-MAIL

NAME

ADDRESS

HOME

MOBILE

WORK / FAX

E-MAIL

NAME

ADDRESS

HOME

MOBILE

WORK / FAX

E-MAIL

NAME

ADDRESS

HOME

MOBILE

WORK / FAX

E-MAIL

NAME

ADDRESS

HOME

MOBILE

WORK / FAX

E-MAIL

NAME

ADDRESS

HOME

MOBILE

WORK / FAX

E-MAIL

NAME

ADDRESS

HOME

MOBILE

WORK / FAX

E-MAIL

NAME

ADDRESS

HOME

MOBILE

WORK / FAX

E-MAIL

NAME

ADDRESS

HOME

MOBILE

WORK / FAX

E-MAIL

NAME

ADDRESS

HOME

MOBILE

WORK / FAX

E-MAIL

NAME

ADDRESS

HOME

MOBILE

WORK / FAX

E-MAIL

NAME

ADDRESS

HOME

MOBILE

WORK / FAX

E-MAIL

NAME

ADDRESS

HOME

MOBILE

WORK / FAX

E-MAIL

NAME

ADDRESS

HOME

MOBILE

WORK / FAX

E-MAIL

NAME

ADDRESS

HOME

MOBILE

WORK / FAX

E-MAIL

NAME

ADDRESS

HOME

MOBILE

WORK / FAX

E-MAIL

NAME

ADDRESS

HOME

MOBILE

WORK / FAX

E-MAIL

NAME

ADDRESS

HOME

MOBILE

WORK / FAX

E-MAIL

NAME

ADDRESS

HOME

MOBILE

WORK / FAX

E-MAIL

NAME

ADDRESS

HOME

MOBILE

WORK / FAX

E-MAIL

NAME

ADDRESS

HOME

MOBILE

WORK / FAX

E-MAIL

NAME

ADDRESS

HOME

MOBILE

WORK / FAX

E-MAIL

NAME

ADDRESS

HOME

MOBILE

WORK / FAX

E-MAIL

NAME

ADDRESS

HOME

MOBILE

WORK / FAX

E-MAIL

NAME

ADDRESS

HOME

MOBILE

WORK / FAX

E-MAIL

NAME

ADDRESS

HOME

MOBILE

WORK / FAX

E-MAIL

NAME

ADDRESS

HOME

MOBILE

WORK / FAX

E-MAIL

NAME

ADDRESS

HOME

MOBILE

WORK / FAX

E-MAIL

NAME

ADDRESS

HOME

MOBILE

WORK / FAX

E-MAIL

NAME

ADDRESS

HOME

MOBILE

WORK / FAX

E-MAIL

NAME

ADDRESS

HOME

MOBILE

WORK / FAX

E-MAIL

NAME

ADDRESS

HOME

MOBILE

WORK / FAX

E-MAIL

NAME

ADDRESS

HOME

MOBILE

WORK / FAX

E-MAIL

NAME

ADDRESS

HOME

MOBILE

WORK / FAX

E-MAIL

NAME

ADDRESS

HOME

MOBILE

WORK / FAX

E-MAIL

NAME

ADDRESS

HOME

MOBILE

WORK / FAX

E-MAIL

NAME

ADDRESS

HOME

MOBILE

WORK / FAX

E-MAIL

NAME

ADDRESS

HOME

MOBILE

WORK / FAX

E-MAIL

NAME

ADDRESS

HOME

MOBILE

WORK / FAX

E-MAIL

NAME

ADDRESS

HOME

MOBILE

WORK / FAX

E-MAIL

NAME

ADDRESS

HOME

MOBILE

WORK / FAX

E-MAIL

NAME

ADDRESS

HOME

MOBILE

WORK / FAX

E-MAIL

NAME

ADDRESS

HOME

MOBILE

WORK / FAX

E-MAIL

NAME

ADDRESS

HOME

MOBILE

WORK / FAX

E-MAIL

NAME

ADDRESS

HOME

MOBILE

WORK / FAX

E-MAIL

NAME

ADDRESS

HOME

MOBILE

WORK / FAX

E-MAIL

NAME

ADDRESS

HOME

MOBILE

WORK / FAX

E-MAIL

NAME

ADDRESS

HOME

MOBILE

WORK / FAX

E-MAIL

NAME

ADDRESS

HOME

MOBILE

WORK / FAX

E-MAIL

NAME

ADDRESS

HOME

MOBILE

WORK / FAX

E-MAIL

NAME

ADDRESS

HOME

MOBILE

WORK / FAX

E-MAIL

NAME

ADDRESS

HOME

MOBILE

WORK / FAX

E-MAIL

NAME

ADDRESS

HOME

MOBILE

WORK / FAX

E-MAIL

NAME

ADDRESS

HOME

MOBILE

WORK / FAX

E-MAIL

NAME

ADDRESS

HOME

MOBILE

WORK / FAX

E-MAIL

NAME

ADDRESS

HOME

MOBILE

WORK / FAX

E-MAIL

NAME

ADDRESS

HOME

MOBILE

WORK / FAX

E-MAIL

NAME

ADDRESS

HOME

MOBILE

WORK / FAX

E-MAIL

NAME

ADDRESS

HOME

MOBILE

WORK / FAX

E-MAIL

NAME

ADDRESS

HOME

MOBILE

WORK / FAX

E-MAIL

NAME

ADDRESS

HOME

MOBILE

WORK / FAX

E-MAIL

NAME

ADDRESS

HOME

MOBILE

WORK / FAX

E-MAIL

NAME

ADDRESS

HOME

MOBILE

WORK / FAX

E-MAIL

NAME

ADDRESS

HOME

MOBILE

WORK / FAX

E-MAIL

NAME

ADDRESS

HOME

MOBILE

WORK / FAX

E-MAIL

NAME

ADDRESS

HOME

MOBILE

WORK / FAX

E-MAIL

NAME

ADDRESS

HOME

MOBILE

WORK / FAX

E-MAIL

NAME

ADDRESS

HOME

MOBILE

WORK / FAX

E-MAIL

NAME

ADDRESS

HOME

MOBILE

WORK / FAX

E-MAIL

NAME

ADDRESS

HOME

MOBILE

WORK / FAX

E-MAIL

NAME

ADDRESS

HOME

MOBILE

WORK / FAX

E-MAIL

NAME

ADDRESS

HOME

MOBILE

WORK / FAX

E-MAIL

NAME

ADDRESS

HOME

MOBILE

WORK / FAX

E-MAIL

NAME

ADDRESS

HOME

MOBILE

WORK / FAX

E-MAIL

NAME

ADDRESS

HOME

MOBILE

WORK / FAX

E-MAIL

NAME

ADDRESS

HOME

MOBILE

WORK / FAX

E-MAIL

NAME

ADDRESS

HOME

MOBILE

WORK / FAX

E-MAIL

NAME

ADDRESS

HOME

MOBILE

WORK / FAX

E-MAIL

NAME

ADDRESS

HOME

MOBILE

WORK / FAX

E-MAIL

NAME

ADDRESS

HOME

MOBILE

WORK / FAX

E-MAIL

NAME

ADDRESS

HOME

MOBILE

WORK / FAX

E-MAIL

NAME

ADDRESS

HOME

MOBILE

WORK / FAX

E-MAIL

NAME

ADDRESS

HOME

MOBILE

WORK / FAX

E-MAIL

NAME

ADDRESS

HOME

MOBILE

WORK / FAX

E-MAIL

NAME

ADDRESS

HOME

MOBILE

WORK / FAX

E-MAIL

NAME

ADDRESS

HOME

MOBILE

WORK / FAX

E-MAIL

NAME

ADDRESS

HOME

MOBILE

WORK / FAX

E-MAIL

NAME

ADDRESS

HOME

MOBILE

WORK / FAX

E-MAIL

NAME

ADDRESS

HOME

MOBILE

WORK / FAX

E-MAIL

NAME

ADDRESS

HOME

MOBILE

WORK / FAX

E-MAIL

NAME

ADDRESS

HOME

MOBILE

WORK / FAX

E-MAIL

NAME

ADDRESS

HOME

MOBILE

WORK / FAX

E-MAIL

NAME

ADDRESS

HOME

MOBILE

WORK / FAX

E-MAIL

NAME

ADDRESS

HOME

MOBILE

WORK / FAX

E-MAIL

NAME

ADDRESS

HOME

MOBILE

WORK / FAX

E-MAIL

NAME

ADDRESS

HOME

MOBILE

WORK / FAX

E-MAIL

NAME

ADDRESS

HOME

MOBILE

WORK / FAX

E-MAIL

NAME

ADDRESS

HOME

MOBILE

WORK / FAX

E-MAIL

NAME

ADDRESS

HOME

MOBILE

WORK / FAX

E-MAIL

G
H

NAME

ADDRESS

HOME

MOBILE

WORK / FAX

E-MAIL

NAME

ADDRESS

HOME

MOBILE

WORK / FAX

E-MAIL

NAME

ADDRESS

HOME

MOBILE

WORK / FAX

E-MAIL

NAME

ADDRESS

HOME

MOBILE

WORK / FAX

E-MAIL

NAME

ADDRESS

HOME

MOBILE

WORK / FAX

E-MAIL

NAME

ADDRESS

HOME

MOBILE

WORK / FAX

E-MAIL

NAME

ADDRESS

HOME

MOBILE

WORK / FAX

E-MAIL

NAME

ADDRESS

HOME

MOBILE

WORK / FAX

E-MAIL

NAME

ADDRESS

HOME

MOBILE

WORK / FAX

E-MAIL

NAME

ADDRESS

HOME

MOBILE

WORK / FAX

E-MAIL

NAME

ADDRESS

HOME

MOBILE

WORK / FAX

E-MAIL

NAME

ADDRESS

HOME

MOBILE

WORK / FAX

E-MAIL

NAME

ADDRESS

HOME

MOBILE

WORK / FAX

E-MAIL

NAME

ADDRESS

HOME

MOBILE

WORK / FAX

E-MAIL

NAME

ADDRESS

HOME

MOBILE

WORK / FAX

E-MAIL

NAME

ADDRESS

HOME

MOBILE

WORK / FAX

E-MAIL

NAME

ADDRESS

HOME

MOBILE

WORK / FAX

E-MAIL

NAME

ADDRESS

HOME

MOBILE

WORK / FAX

E-MAIL

NAME

ADDRESS

HOME

MOBILE

WORK / FAX

E-MAIL

NAME

ADDRESS

HOME

MOBILE

WORK / FAX

E-MAIL

NAME

ADDRESS

HOME

MOBILE

WORK / FAX

E-MAIL

NAME

ADDRESS

HOME

MOBILE

WORK / FAX

E-MAIL

NAME

ADDRESS

HOME

MOBILE

WORK / FAX

E-MAIL

NAME

ADDRESS

HOME

MOBILE

WORK / FAX

E-MAIL

NAME

ADDRESS

HOME

MOBILE

WORK / FAX

E-MAIL

NAME

ADDRESS

HOME

MOBILE

WORK / FAX

E-MAIL

NAME

ADDRESS

HOME

MOBILE

WORK / FAX

E-MAIL

NAME

ADDRESS

HOME

MOBILE

WORK / FAX

E-MAIL

NAME

ADDRESS

HOME

MOBILE

WORK / FAX

E-MAIL

NAME

ADDRESS

HOME

MOBILE

WORK / FAX

E-MAIL

NAME

ADDRESS

HOME

MOBILE

WORK / FAX

E-MAIL

NAME

ADDRESS

HOME

MOBILE

WORK / FAX

E-MAIL

NAME

ADDRESS

HOME

MOBILE

WORK / FAX

E-MAIL

NAME

ADDRESS

HOME

MOBILE

WORK / FAX

E-MAIL

NAME

ADDRESS

HOME

MOBILE

WORK / FAX

E-MAIL

NAME

ADDRESS

HOME

MOBILE

WORK / FAX

E-MAIL

NAME

ADDRESS

HOME

MOBILE

WORK / FAX

E-MAIL

NAME

ADDRESS

HOME

MOBILE

WORK / FAX

E-MAIL

NAME

ADDRESS

HOME

MOBILE

WORK / FAX

E-MAIL

NAME

ADDRESS

HOME

MOBILE

WORK / FAX

E-MAIL

NAME

ADDRESS

HOME

MOBILE

WORK / FAX

E-MAIL

NAME

ADDRESS

HOME

MOBILE

WORK / FAX

E-MAIL

NAME

ADDRESS

HOME

MOBILE

WORK / FAX

E-MAIL

NAME

ADDRESS

HOME

MOBILE

WORK / FAX

E-MAIL

NAME

ADDRESS

HOME

MOBILE

WORK / FAX

E-MAIL

NAME

ADDRESS

HOME

MOBILE

WORK / FAX

E-MAIL

NAME

ADDRESS

HOME

MOBILE

WORK / FAX

E-MAIL

NAME

ADDRESS

HOME

MOBILE

WORK / FAX

E-MAIL

NAME

ADDRESS

HOME

MOBILE

WORK / FAX

E-MAIL

NAME

ADDRESS

HOME

MOBILE

WORK / FAX

E-MAIL

NAME

ADDRESS

HOME

MOBILE

WORK / FAX

E-MAIL

NAME

ADDRESS

HOME

MOBILE

WORK / FAX

E-MAIL

NAME

ADDRESS

HOME

MOBILE

WORK / FAX

E-MAIL

NAME

ADDRESS

HOME

MOBILE

WORK / FAX

E-MAIL

NAME

ADDRESS

HOME

MOBILE

WORK / FAX

E-MAIL

NAME

ADDRESS

HOME

MOBILE

WORK / FAX

E-MAIL

NAME

ADDRESS

HOME

MOBILE

WORK / FAX

E-MAIL

NAME

ADDRESS

HOME

MOBILE

WORK / FAX

E-MAIL

NAME

ADDRESS

HOME

MOBILE

WORK / FAX

E-MAIL

NAME

ADDRESS

HOME

MOBILE

WORK / FAX

E-MAIL

NAME

ADDRESS

HOME

MOBILE

WORK / FAX

E-MAIL

NAME

ADDRESS

HOME

MOBILE

WORK / FAX

E-MAIL

NAME

ADDRESS

HOME

MOBILE

WORK / FAX

E-MAIL

NAME

ADDRESS

HOME

MOBILE

WORK / FAX

E-MAIL

NAME

ADDRESS

HOME

MOBILE

WORK / FAX

E-MAIL

NAME

ADDRESS

HOME

MOBILE

WORK / FAX

E-MAIL

NAME

ADDRESS

HOME

MOBILE

WORK / FAX

E-MAIL

NAME

ADDRESS

HOME

MOBILE

WORK / FAX

E-MAIL

NAME

ADDRESS

HOME

MOBILE

WORK / FAX

E-MAIL

NAME

ADDRESS

HOME

MOBILE

WORK / FAX

E-MAIL

NAME

ADDRESS

HOME

MOBILE

WORK / FAX

E-MAIL

NAME

ADDRESS

HOME

MOBILE

WORK / FAX

E-MAIL

NAME

ADDRESS

HOME

MOBILE

WORK / FAX

E-MAIL

NAME

ADDRESS

HOME

MOBILE

WORK / FAX

E-MAIL

NAME

ADDRESS

HOME

MOBILE

WORK / FAX

E-MAIL

NAME

ADDRESS

HOME

MOBILE

WORK / FAX

E-MAIL

NAME

ADDRESS

HOME

MOBILE

WORK / FAX

E-MAIL

NAME

ADDRESS

HOME

MOBILE

WORK / FAX

E-MAIL

NAME

ADDRESS

HOME

MOBILE

WORK / FAX

E-MAIL

NAME

ADDRESS

HOME

MOBILE

WORK / FAX

E-MAIL

NAME

ADDRESS

HOME

MOBILE

WORK / FAX

E-MAIL

NAME

ADDRESS

HOME

MOBILE

WORK / FAX

E-MAIL

NAME

ADDRESS

HOME

MOBILE

WORK / FAX

E-MAIL

NAME

ADDRESS

HOME

MOBILE

WORK / FAX

E-MAIL

NAME

ADDRESS

HOME

MOBILE

WORK / FAX

E-MAIL

NAME

ADDRESS

HOME

MOBILE

WORK / FAX

E-MAIL

NAME

ADDRESS

HOME

MOBILE

WORK / FAX

E-MAIL

NAME

ADDRESS

HOME

MOBILE

WORK / FAX

E-MAIL

NAME

ADDRESS

HOME

MOBILE

WORK / FAX

E-MAIL

NAME

ADDRESS

HOME

MOBILE

WORK / FAX

E-MAIL

NAME

ADDRESS

HOME

MOBILE

WORK / FAX

E-MAIL

NAME

ADDRESS

HOME

MOBILE

WORK / FAX

E-MAIL

NAME

ADDRESS

HOME

MOBILE

WORK / FAX

E-MAIL

NAME

ADDRESS

HOME

MOBILE

WORK / FAX

E-MAIL

NAME

ADDRESS

HOME

MOBILE

WORK / FAX

E-MAIL

NAME

ADDRESS

HOME

MOBILE

WORK / FAX

E-MAIL

NAME

ADDRESS

K
L

HOME

MOBILE

WORK / FAX

E-MAIL

NAME

ADDRESS

HOME

MOBILE

WORK / FAX

E-MAIL

NAME

ADDRESS

HOME

MOBILE

WORK / FAX

E-MAIL

NAME

ADDRESS

HOME

MOBILE

WORK / FAX

E-MAIL

NAME

ADDRESS

HOME

MOBILE

WORK / FAX

E-MAIL

NAME

ADDRESS

HOME

MOBILE

WORK / FAX

E-MAIL

NAME

ADDRESS

HOME

MOBILE

WORK / FAX

E-MAIL

NAME

ADDRESS

HOME

MOBILE

WORK / FAX

E-MAIL

NAME

ADDRESS

HOME

MOBILE

WORK / FAX

E-MAIL

NAME

ADDRESS

HOME

MOBILE

WORK / FAX

E-MAIL

NAME

ADDRESS

HOME

MOBILE

WORK / FAX

E-MAIL

NAME

ADDRESS

HOME

MOBILE

WORK / FAX

E-MAIL

NAME

ADDRESS

HOME

MOBILE

WORK / FAX

E-MAIL

NAME

ADDRESS

HOME

MOBILE

WORK / FAX

E-MAIL

NAME

ADDRESS

HOME

MOBILE

WORK / FAX

E-MAIL

NAME

ADDRESS

HOME

MOBILE

WORK / FAX

E-MAIL

NAME

ADDRESS

HOME

MOBILE

WORK / FAX

E-MAIL

NAME

ADDRESS

HOME

MOBILE

WORK / FAX

E-MAIL

NAME

ADDRESS

HOME

MOBILE

WORK / FAX

E-MAIL

NAME

ADDRESS

HOME

MOBILE

WORK / FAX

E-MAIL

NAME

ADDRESS

HOME

MOBILE

WORK / FAX

E-MAIL

NAME

ADDRESS

HOME

MOBILE

WORK / FAX

E-MAIL

NAME

ADDRESS

HOME

MOBILE

WORK / FAX

E-MAIL

NAME

ADDRESS

HOME

MOBILE

WORK / FAX

E-MAIL

NAME

ADDRESS

HOME

MOBILE

WORK / FAX

E-MAIL

NAME

ADDRESS

HOME

MOBILE

WORK / FAX

E-MAIL

NAME

ADDRESS

HOME

MOBILE

WORK / FAX

E-MAIL

NAME

ADDRESS

HOME

MOBILE

WORK / FAX

E-MAIL

NAME

ADDRESS

HOME

MOBILE

WORK / FAX

E-MAIL

NAME

ADDRESS

HOME

MOBILE

WORK / FAX

E-MAIL

NAME

ADDRESS

HOME

MOBILE

WORK / FAX

E-MAIL

NAME

ADDRESS

HOME

MOBILE

WORK / FAX

E-MAIL

NAME

ADDRESS

HOME

MOBILE

WORK / FAX

E-MAIL

NAME

ADDRESS

HOME

MOBILE

WORK / FAX

E-MAIL

NAME

ADDRESS

HOME

MOBILE

WORK / FAX

E-MAIL

NAME

ADDRESS

HOME

MOBILE

WORK / FAX

E-MAIL

NAME

ADDRESS

HOME

MOBILE

WORK / FAX

E-MAIL

NAME

ADDRESS

HOME

MOBILE

WORK / FAX

E-MAIL

NAME

ADDRESS

HOME

MOBILE

WORK / FAX

E-MAIL

NAME

ADDRESS

HOME

MOBILE

WORK / FAX

E-MAIL

NAME

ADDRESS

HOME

MOBILE

WORK / FAX

E-MAIL

NAME

ADDRESS

HOME

MOBILE

WORK / FAX

E-MAIL

NAME

ADDRESS

HOME

MOBILE

WORK / FAX

E-MAIL

NAME

ADDRESS

HOME

MOBILE

WORK / FAX

E-MAIL

NAME

ADDRESS

HOME

MOBILE

WORK / FAX

E-MAIL

NAME

ADDRESS

HOME

MOBILE

WORK / FAX

E-MAIL

NAME

ADDRESS

HOME

MOBILE

WORK / FAX

E-MAIL

NAME

ADDRESS

HOME

MOBILE

WORK / FAX

E-MAIL

NAME

ADDRESS

HOME

MOBILE

WORK / FAX

E-MAIL

NAME

ADDRESS

HOME

MOBILE

WORK / FAX

E-MAIL

NAME

ADDRESS

HOME

MOBILE

WORK / FAX

E-MAIL

NAME

ADDRESS

HOME

MOBILE

WORK / FAX

E-MAIL

NAME

ADDRESS

HOME

MOBILE

WORK / FAX

E-MAIL

NAME

ADDRESS

HOME

MOBILE

WORK / FAX

E-MAIL

NAME

ADDRESS

HOME

MOBILE

WORK / FAX

E-MAIL

NAME

ADDRESS

HOME

MOBILE

WORK / FAX

E-MAIL

NAME

ADDRESS

HOME

MOBILE

WORK / FAX

E-MAIL

NAME

ADDRESS

HOME

MOBILE

WORK / FAX

E-MAIL

NAME

ADDRESS

HOME

MOBILE

WORK / FAX

E-MAIL

NAME

ADDRESS

HOME

MOBILE

WORK / FAX

E-MAIL

NAME

ADDRESS

HOME

MOBILE

WORK / FAX

E-MAIL

NAME

ADDRESS

HOME

MOBILE

WORK / FAX

E-MAIL

NAME

ADDRESS

HOME

MOBILE

WORK / FAX

E-MAIL

NAME

ADDRESS

HOME

MOBILE

WORK / FAX

E-MAIL

NAME

ADDRESS

HOME

MOBILE

WORK / FAX

E-MAIL

NAME

ADDRESS

HOME

MOBILE

WORK / FAX

E-MAIL

NAME

ADDRESS

HOME

MOBILE

WORK / FAX

E-MAIL

NAME

ADDRESS

HOME

MOBILE

WORK / FAX

E-MAIL

NAME

ADDRESS

HOME

MOBILE

WORK / FAX

E-MAIL

NAME

ADDRESS

HOME

MOBILE

WORK / FAX

E-MAIL

NAME

ADDRESS

HOME

MOBILE

WORK / FAX

E-MAIL

NAME

ADDRESS

HOME

MOBILE

WORK / FAX

E-MAIL

NAME

ADDRESS

HOME

MOBILE

WORK / FAX

E-MAIL

NAME

ADDRESS

HOME

MOBILE

WORK / FAX

E-MAIL

NAME

ADDRESS

HOME

MOBILE

WORK / FAX

E-MAIL

NAME

ADDRESS

HOME

MOBILE

WORK / FAX

E-MAIL

NAME

ADDRESS

HOME

MOBILE

WORK / FAX

E-MAIL

NAME

ADDRESS

HOME

MOBILE

WORK / FAX

E-MAIL

NAME

ADDRESS

HOME

MOBILE

WORK / FAX

E-MAIL

NAME

ADDRESS

HOME

MOBILE

WORK / FAX

E-MAIL

NAME

ADDRESS

HOME

MOBILE

WORK / FAX

E-MAIL

NAME

ADDRESS

HOME

MOBILE

WORK / FAX

E-MAIL

NAME

ADDRESS

HOME

MOBILE

WORK / FAX

E-MAIL

NAME

ADDRESS

HOME

MOBILE

WORK / FAX

E-MAIL

NAME

ADDRESS

HOME

MOBILE

WORK / FAX

E-MAIL

NAME

ADDRESS

HOME

MOBILE

WORK / FAX

E-MAIL

NAME

ADDRESS

HOME

MOBILE

WORK / FAX

E-MAIL

NAME

ADDRESS

HOME

MOBILE

WORK / FAX

E-MAIL

NAME

ADDRESS

HOME

MOBILE

WORK / FAX

E-MAIL

NAME

ADDRESS

HOME

MOBILE

WORK / FAX

E-MAIL

NAME

ADDRESS

HOME

MOBILE

WORK / FAX

E-MAIL

NAME

ADDRESS

HOME

MOBILE

WORK / FAX

E-MAIL

NAME

ADDRESS

HOME

MOBILE

WORK / FAX

E-MAIL

NAME

ADDRESS

HOME

MOBILE

WORK / FAX

E-MAIL

NAME

ADDRESS

HOME

MOBILE

WORK / FAX

E-MAIL

NAME

ADDRESS

HOME

MOBILE

WORK / FAX

E-MAIL

NAME

ADDRESS

HOME

MOBILE

WORK / FAX

E-MAIL

NAME

ADDRESS

HOME

MOBILE

WORK / FAX

E-MAIL

NAME

ADDRESS

HOME

MOBILE

WORK / FAX

E-MAIL

NAME

ADDRESS

HOME

MOBILE

WORK / FAX

E-MAIL

NAME

ADDRESS

HOME

MOBILE

WORK / FAX

E-MAIL

NAME

ADDRESS

HOME

MOBILE

WORK / FAX

E-MAIL

NAME

ADDRESS

HOME

MOBILE

WORK / FAX

E-MAIL

NAME

ADDRESS

HOME

MOBILE

WORK / FAX

E-MAIL

NAME

ADDRESS

HOME

MOBILE

WORK / FAX

E-MAIL

NAME

ADDRESS

HOME

MOBILE

WORK / FAX

E-MAIL

NAME

ADDRESS

HOME

MOBILE

WORK / FAX

E-MAIL

NAME

ADDRESS

HOME

MOBILE

WORK / FAX

E-MAIL

NAME

ADDRESS

HOME

MOBILE

WORK / FAX

E-MAIL

NAME

ADDRESS

HOME

MOBILE

WORK / FAX

E-MAIL

NAME D.J. Skopelitis

ADDRESS

HOME

MOBILE (732) 779-9493

WORK / FAX

E-MAIL

NAME

ADDRESS

HOME

MOBILE

WORK / FAX

E-MAIL

NAME

ADDRESS

HOME

MOBILE

WORK / FAX

E-MAIL

NAME Barry & Connie Lee Thatcher

ADDRESS 3578 Beufort Court

Naples, Florida 34119

HOME

MOBILE Connie (732) 773-5436

WORK / FAX

E-MAIL

NAME

ADDRESS

HOME

MOBILE

WORK / FAX

E-MAIL

NAME

ADDRESS

HOME

MOBILE

WORK / FAX

E-MAIL

NAME

ADDRESS

HOME

MOBILE

WORK / FAX

E-MAIL

NAME

ADDRESS

HOME

MOBILE

WORK / FAX

E-MAIL

NAME

ADDRESS

HOME

MOBILE

WORK / FAX

E-MAIL

NAME

ADDRESS

HOME

MOBILE

WORK / FAX

E-MAIL

NAME

ADDRESS

HOME

MOBILE

WORK / FAX

E-MAIL

NAME

ADDRESS

HOME

MOBILE

WORK / FAX

E-MAIL

NAME

ADDRESS

HOME

MOBILE

WORK / FAX

E-MAIL

NAME

ADDRESS

HOME

MOBILE

WORK / FAX

E-MAIL

NAME

ADDRESS

HOME

MOBILE

WORK / FAX

E-MAIL

NAME

ADDRESS

HOME

MOBILE

WORK / FAX

E-MAIL

NAME

ADDRESS

HOME

MOBILE

WORK / FAX

E-MAIL

NAME

ADDRESS

HOME

MOBILE

WORK / FAX

E-MAIL

NAME

ADDRESS

HOME

MOBILE

WORK / FAX

E-MAIL

NAME

ADDRESS

HOME

MOBILE

WORK / FAX

E-MAIL

NAME

ADDRESS

HOME

MOBILE

WORK / FAX

E-MAIL

NAME

ADDRESS

HOME

MOBILE

WORK / FAX

E-MAIL

NAME

ADDRESS

HOME

MOBILE

WORK / FAX

E-MAIL

NAME

ADDRESS

HOME

MOBILE

WORK / FAX

E-MAIL

NAME

ADDRESS

HOME

MOBILE

WORK / FAX

E-MAIL

NAME

ADDRESS

HOME

MOBILE

WORK / FAX

E-MAIL

NAME

ADDRESS

HOME

MOBILE

WORK / FAX

E-MAIL

NAME

ADDRESS

HOME

MOBILE

WORK / FAX

E-MAIL

NAME

ADDRESS

HOME

MOBILE

WORK / FAX

E-MAIL

NAME

ADDRESS

HOME

MOBILE

WORK / FAX

E-MAIL

NAME

ADDRESS

HOME

MOBILE

WORK / FAX

E-MAIL

NAME

ADDRESS

HOME

MOBILE

WORK / FAX

E-MAIL

NAME

ADDRESS

HOME

MOBILE

WORK / FAX

E-MAIL

NAME

ADDRESS

HOME

MOBILE

WORK / FAX

E-MAIL

NAME

ADDRESS

HOME

MOBILE

WORK / FAX

E-MAIL

NAME

ADDRESS

HOME

MOBILE

WORK / FAX

E-MAIL

NAME

ADDRESS

HOME

MOBILE

WORK / FAX

E-MAIL

NAME

ADDRESS

HOME

MOBILE

WORK / FAX

E-MAIL

NAME

ADDRESS

HOME

MOBILE

WORK / FAX

E-MAIL

NAME

ADDRESS

HOME

MOBILE

WORK / FAX

E-MAIL

NAME

ADDRESS

HOME

MOBILE

WORK / FAX

E-MAIL

NAME

ADDRESS

HOME

MOBILE

WORK / FAX

E-MAIL

NAME

ADDRESS

HOME

MOBILE

WORK / FAX

E-MAIL

NAME

ADDRESS

HOME

MOBILE

WORK / FAX

E-MAIL

NAME

ADDRESS

HOME

MOBILE

WORK / FAX

E-MAIL

NAME

ADDRESS

HOME

MOBILE

WORK / FAX

E-MAIL

NAME

ADDRESS

HOME

MOBILE

WORK / FAX

E-MAIL

NAME

ADDRESS

HOME

MOBILE

WORK / FAX

E-MAIL

NAME

ADDRESS

HOME

MOBILE

WORK / FAX

E-MAIL

NAME

ADDRESS

HOME

MOBILE

WORK / FAX

E-MAIL

NAME

ADDRESS

HOME

MOBILE

WORK / FAX

E-MAIL

NAME

ADDRESS

HOME

MOBILE

WORK / FAX

E-MAIL

NAME

ADDRESS

HOME

MOBILE

WORK / FAX

E-MAIL

NAME

ADDRESS

HOME

MOBILE

WORK / FAX

E-MAIL

U
V

NAME

ADDRESS

HOME

MOBILE

WORK / FAX

E-MAIL

NAME

ADDRESS

HOME

MOBILE

WORK / FAX

E-MAIL

NAME

ADDRESS

HOME

MOBILE

WORK / FAX

E-MAIL

NAME

ADDRESS

HOME

MOBILE

WORK / FAX

E-MAIL

NAME

ADDRESS

HOME

MOBILE

WORK / FAX

E-MAIL

NAME

ADDRESS

HOME

MOBILE

WORK / FAX

E-MAIL

NAME

ADDRESS

HOME

MOBILE

WORK / FAX

E-MAIL

NAME

ADDRESS

HOME

MOBILE

WORK / FAX

E-MAIL

NAME

ADDRESS

HOME

MOBILE

WORK / FAX

E-MAIL

NAME

ADDRESS

HOME

MOBILE

WORK / FAX

E-MAIL

NAME

ADDRESS

HOME

MOBILE

WORK / FAX

E-MAIL

NAME

ADDRESS

HOME

MOBILE

WORK / FAX

E-MAIL

NAME

ADDRESS

HOME

MOBILE

WORK / FAX

E-MAIL

NAME

ADDRESS

HOME

MOBILE

WORK / FAX

E-MAIL

NAME

ADDRESS

HOME

MOBILE

WORK / FAX

E-MAIL

NAME

ADDRESS

HOME

MOBILE

WORK / FAX

E-MAIL

NAME

ADDRESS

HOME

MOBILE

WORK / FAX

E-MAIL

NAME

ADDRESS

HOME

MOBILE

WORK / FAX

E-MAIL

NAME

ADDRESS

HOME

MOBILE

WORK / FAX

E-MAIL

NAME

ADDRESS

HOME

MOBILE

WORK / FAX

E-MAIL

NAME

ADDRESS

HOME

MOBILE

WORK / FAX

E-MAIL

NAME

ADDRESS

HOME

MOBILE

WORK / FAX

E-MAIL

NAME

ADDRESS

HOME

MOBILE

WORK / FAX

E-MAIL

NAME

ADDRESS

HOME

MOBILE

WORK / FAX

E-MAIL

W
X

NAME

ADDRESS

HOME

MOBILE

WORK / FAX

E-MAIL

NAME

ADDRESS

HOME

MOBILE

WORK / FAX

E-MAIL

NAME

ADDRESS

HOME

MOBILE

WORK / FAX

E-MAIL

NAME

ADDRESS

HOME

MOBILE

WORK / FAX

E-MAIL

NAME

ADDRESS

HOME

MOBILE

WORK / FAX

E-MAIL

NAME

ADDRESS

HOME

MOBILE

WORK / FAX

E-MAIL

W
X

NAME

ADDRESS

HOME

MOBILE

WORK / FAX

E-MAIL

NAME

ADDRESS

HOME

MOBILE

WORK / FAX

E-MAIL

NAME

ADDRESS

HOME

MOBILE

WORK / FAX

E-MAIL

NAME

ADDRESS

HOME

MOBILE

WORK / FAX

E-MAIL

NAME

ADDRESS

HOME

MOBILE

WORK / FAX

E-MAIL

NAME

ADDRESS

HOME

MOBILE

WORK / FAX

E-MAIL

NAME

ADDRESS

HOME

MOBILE

WORK / FAX

E-MAIL

NAME

ADDRESS

HOME

MOBILE

WORK / FAX

E-MAIL

NAME

ADDRESS

HOME

MOBILE

WORK / FAX

E-MAIL

NAME

ADDRESS

HOME

MOBILE

WORK / FAX

E-MAIL

NAME

ADDRESS

HOME

MOBILE

WORK / FAX

E-MAIL

NAME

ADDRESS

HOME

MOBILE

WORK / FAX

E-MAIL

NAME

ADDRESS

HOME

MOBILE

WORK / FAX

E-MAIL

NAME

ADDRESS

HOME

MOBILE

WORK / FAX

E-MAIL

NAME

ADDRESS

HOME

MOBILE

WORK / FAX

E-MAIL

NAME

ADDRESS

HOME

MOBILE

WORK / FAX

E-MAIL

NAME

ADDRESS

HOME

MOBILE

WORK / FAX

E-MAIL

NAME

ADDRESS

HOME

MOBILE

WORK / FAX

E-MAIL

NAME

ADDRESS

HOME

MOBILE

WORK / FAX

E-MAIL

NAME

ADDRESS

HOME

MOBILE

WORK / FAX

E-MAIL

NAME

ADDRESS

HOME

MOBILE

WORK / FAX

E-MAIL

NAME

ADDRESS

HOME

MOBILE

WORK / FAX

E-MAIL

NAME

ADDRESS

HOME

MOBILE

WORK / FAX

E-MAIL

NAME

ADDRESS

HOME

MOBILE

WORK / FAX

E-MAIL

NAME

ADDRESS

HOME

MOBILE

WORK / FAX

E-MAIL

NAME

ADDRESS

HOME

MOBILE

WORK / FAX

E-MAIL

NAME

ADDRESS

HOME

MOBILE

WORK / FAX

E-MAIL

NAME

ADDRESS

HOME

MOBILE

WORK / FAX

E-MAIL

NAME

ADDRESS

HOME

MOBILE

WORK / FAX

E-MAIL

NAME

ADDRESS

HOME

MOBILE

WORK / FAX

E-MAIL

NAME

ADDRESS

HOME

MOBILE

WORK / FAX

E-MAIL

NAME

ADDRESS

HOME

MOBILE

WORK / FAX

E-MAIL

NAME

ADDRESS

HOME

MOBILE

WORK / FAX

E-MAIL

NAME

ADDRESS

HOME

MOBILE

WORK / FAX

E-MAIL

NAME

ADDRESS

HOME

MOBILE

WORK / FAX

E-MAIL

NAME

ADDRESS

HOME

MOBILE

WORK / FAX

E-MAIL

NAME

ADDRESS

HOME

MOBILE

WORK / FAX

E-MAIL

NAME

ADDRESS

HOME

MOBILE

WORK / FAX

E-MAIL

NAME

ADDRESS

HOME

MOBILE

WORK / FAX

E-MAIL

NAME

ADDRESS

HOME

MOBILE

WORK / FAX

E-MAIL

NAME

ADDRESS

HOME

MOBILE

WORK / FAX

E-MAIL

NAME

ADDRESS

HOME

MOBILE

WORK / FAX

E-MAIL

Y
Z

NAME

ADDRESS

HOME

MOBILE

WORK / FAX

E-MAIL

NAME

ADDRESS

HOME

MOBILE

WORK / FAX

E-MAIL

NAME

ADDRESS

HOME

MOBILE

WORK / FAX

E-MAIL

NAME

ADDRESS

HOME

MOBILE

WORK / FAX

E-MAIL

NAME

ADDRESS

HOME

MOBILE

WORK / FAX

E-MAIL

NAME

ADDRESS

HOME

MOBILE

WORK / FAX

E-MAIL

NAME

ADDRESS

HOME

MOBILE

WORK / FAX

E-MAIL

NAME

ADDRESS

HOME

MOBILE

WORK / FAX

E-MAIL

NAME

ADDRESS

HOME

MOBILE

WORK / FAX

E-MAIL

NAME

ADDRESS

HOME

MOBILE

WORK / FAX

E-MAIL

NAME

ADDRESS

HOME

MOBILE

WORK / FAX

E-MAIL

NAME

ADDRESS

HOME

MOBILE

WORK / FAX

E-MAIL

NAME

ADDRESS

HOME

MOBILE

WORK / FAX

E-MAIL

NAME

ADDRESS

HOME

MOBILE

WORK / FAX

E-MAIL

NAME

ADDRESS

HOME

MOBILE

WORK / FAX

E-MAIL

NAME

ADDRESS

HOME

MOBILE

WORK / FAX

E-MAIL

NAME

ADDRESS

HOME

MOBILE

WORK / FAX

E-MAIL

NAME

ADDRESS

HOME

MOBILE

WORK / FAX

E-MAIL